Team Sports
at the Paralympics

BY MATT BOWERS

AMICUS | AMICUS INK

Amicus High Interest and Amicus Ink are published by Amicus
P.O. Box 1329, Mankato, MN 56002
www.amicuspublishing.us

Library of Congress Cataloging-in-Publication Data
Names: Bowers, Matt, author.
Title: Team sports at the Paralympics / by Matt Bowers.
Description: Mankato, Minnesota : Amicus/Amicus Ink, [2020]
  | Series: Paralympic sports | Audience: Grades K–3 |
  Includes index.
Identifiers: LCCN 2018056775 (print) | LCCN 2019004484
  (ebook) | ISBN 9781681518701 (pdf) | ISBN
  9781681518305 (library binding) | ISBN
  9781681525587 (pbk.)
Subjects: LCSH: Paralympic Games—Juvenile literature. | Sports
  for people with disabilities—Juvenile literature. | Athletes with
  disabilities—Juvenile literature. | Team sports—Juvenile
  literature.
Classification: LCC GV722.5.P37 (ebook) | LCC
  GV722.5.P37 B66 2020 (print) | DDC 796.04/56—dc23
LC record available at https://lccn.loc.gov/2018056775

Editor: Alissa Thielges
Series Designer: Kathleen Petelinsek
Book Designer: Ciara Beitlich
Photo Researchers: Holly Young and Shane Freed

Photo Credits: AP/Shen ao - Imaginechina cover; AP/Iliya
Pitalev 5; AP/Jonathan Buckmaster 6; Getty/Christophe Simon
8–9; Getty/Steve Russell 10; Shutterstock/Martynova Anna
13; Alamy/Bob Daemmrich 14, 17, 18–19; Alamy/Gareth
Fuller 20; Alamy/PhotoAbility 22–23; Shutterstock/A.Ricardo
24; Alamy/Nippon News 27; Alamy/Actionplus 28

Printed in the United States of America

HC 10 9 8 7 6 5 4 3 2
PB 10 9 8 7 6 5 4 3 2

Table of Contents

Going for Gold

Two teams face off. They come from different countries. They have **disabilities**, but they are some of the world's best athletes. It's their moment to shine in the Summer Paralympic Games. Team sports require skill, teamwork, and strength. These teams have trained hard. Now they are ready to compete for a gold medal.

 How often are the Summer Paralympic Games?

Iran plays against China in sitting volleyball at the 2016 Paralympics.

 They are every four years. They occur the same year as the Summer Olympics.

Football players rely on sound to move the ball down the field.

Football

The fans are quiet. On the field, four teammates pass the soccer ball. They wear **eyeshades**. They can't see anything. But they can hear. They listen for the ball. It makes noise. They kick the ball towards the goal. One player gets an opening. He kicks. Goal! This is football 5-a-side. It's been in the Paralympics since 2004.

 Only after a goal is scored. Otherwise they must stay quiet so the players can hear the ball.

In the United States, football is called soccer. But many other countries call it football. The Paralympics call it football, too. The field and goals are smaller than those in Olympic football. The team with the most goals wins. Brazil is the team to beat. They have won every Paralympic gold medal since 2004.

A Brazilian player kicks the ball around his Turkish opponent.

Mexico's goalie (blue) gets ready to save the ball before it goes in the net.

 How do players know where to kick the ball?

In football 5-a-side, players have a visual **impairment**. Only men compete in this event. Each team has five players on the field. The goalie is able to see. The other four wear eyeshades. This keeps the game fair. The ball has bells in it. This helps players know where it is. Walls keep the ball and players inside the field.

 They listen to their team's guide and coach who shout from the sidelines. Goalies can help them, too.

The 2016 Paralympics had two types of football: 5-a-side and 7-a-side. Football 7-a-side has teams of seven. Athletes with balance and muscle impairments play this sport. However, football 7-a-side will not be in the 2020 Paralympics. It was dropped because not enough countries have an **elite** team. Only football 5-a-side will be played in 2020.

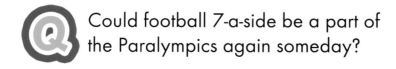 Could football 7-a-side be a part of the Paralympics again someday?

Great Britain (blue) and Russia compete in 7-a-side football in 2012.

 If there are enough elite teams, yes.

Team members from Iran (green) try to block a hit from Brazil.

Q What is the height of the net in sitting volleyball?

Sitting Volleyball

The volleyball is served. It flies over the net. A team of six works together. They are all sitting on the court. One teammate bumps the ball. Another hits it. A third player **spikes** it. The ball rockets over the net. It lands on the other side of the court. One point! Sitting volleyball is filled with excitement and fast plays.

 For men, the top of the net is 1.15 meters (3.8 feet) high. For women, it is 1.05 meters (3.4 feet) high.

Paralympic volleyball players all have a physical impairment. This affects their ability to move around. Some players may be an **amputee** or have a missing limb. Other players may have an impaired muscle or joint. It could be from an injury or a condition. This impacts an athlete's strength or flexibility.

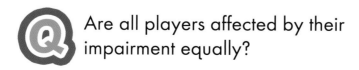

Are all players affected by their impairment equally?

A U.S. player sets the ball to her teammate.

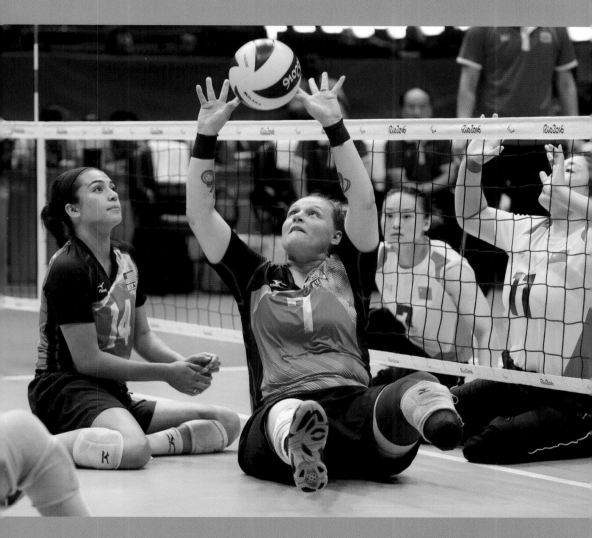

 No. Some players are **minimally impaired**. A team can have two of these players.

Sitting volleyball uses a smaller court than Olympic volleyball. The net is also lower. This is because the players must stay seated on the floor. Players use their hands to move around quickly. A team gets three hits to send the ball back over the net.

Egypt (red) works to overcome Germany's lead in the 2016 Paralympics.

Players use their bodies to
stop the ball in goalball.

Goalball

Three goalball teammates are side by side.
They are on their hands and knees, ready
to move. They wear eyeshades. On the
other side of the court, an opponent hurls
a noisy ball. It zooms down the court. The
teammates lunge. They try to stop the ball
before it goes into the goal behind them.
This is goalball!

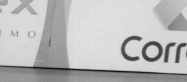

In goalball, players are visually impaired. To keep the game fair, they wear eyeshades. There are two teams. Each has three players on the court at one time. String is taped to the lines of the court. Players feel the string. This helps them know where they are on the court.

A player from Australia winds up to throw the ball down the court.

Padded pants and elbow pads protect the players as they dive to stop the ball.

 How wide and tall are the goals in goalball?

Teams try to throw the ball into the other team's goal. They also defend their goal. They try to block the ball as it rolls toward them. The goals span the width of the court. That's a big area to defend! During the game, fans keep quiet. This helps players listen for the ball.

 The goals are 9 meters (29.5 feet) wide by 1.3 meters (4.3 feet) tall.

Goalball games are 24 minutes long. Before the game there is a coin toss. The team that wins the toss picks whether they throw or defend first. Or they can pick which side they want to start on. At halftime, they switch sides. The team with the most points wins the game. Another way to win is to lead the other team by ten points. Then the game ends early and the team in the lead wins.

Israel scores a point in a game against Japan (red).

Turkey's men's goalball team celebrates their bronze medal in the 2012 Paralympics.

The Next Paralympics

Paralympic football, sitting volleyball, and goalball are not to be missed. Other Paralympic sports can be played in teams, too, like rowing and wheelchair basketball. Tokyo, Japan, will host the Paralympics in 2020. Outstanding teams will compete. Only the best will win a medal. Don't miss these exciting sports!

Glossary

amputee A person who has had a limb, usually an arm or a leg, removed from his or her body.

disability A physical or mental condition that limits a person's movements, senses, or activities.

elite The top level of competition in a sport where you can compete internationally.

eyeshade Sports equipment that covers the eyes completely.

goalie A football player who defends the goal.

impairment A difference in a person's body structure or function or mental function.

minimally impaired An athlete whose impairment doesn't impact their play of the sport very much but may stop them from competing in able-bodied sports.

spike To hit a volleyball over the net in a downward direction using the palm of your hand.

Read More

Fullman, Joe. *Going for Gold: A Guide to the Summer Games*. London: Wayland, 2016.

Osborne, M. K. *Volleyball*. Summer Olympic Sports. Mankato, Minn.: Amicus, 2020.

Websites

International Blind Sports Federation | Football—General Information
http://www.ibsasport.org/sports/football/

Olympics | Paralympic Games: History
https://www.olympic.org/paralympic-games

Tokyo 2020 | The Games: Paralympic Sports
https://tokyo2020.org/en/games/sport/paralympic/

Index

About the Author

Matt Bowers is a writer and illustrator who lives in Minnesota. When he's not writing or drawing, he enjoys skiing, sailing, and going on adventures with his family. As a sports fan, he looks forward to the 2020 Paralympic Games in Tokyo, Japan!